# Know Your Woodpigeon Shooting

by Denis Graham-Hogg

# *The British Association for Shooting & Conservation*

The Association was founded in 1908 by Stanley Duncan, F.Z.S., (Hon.) as the Wildfowler's Association of Great Britain and Ireland. He became and remained for 40 years, its first Honorary Secretary. Also responsible for the Association's founding was Sir Ralph Payne-Gallwey, Bt., who became its first President. Both men realised that unless steps were taken to form an influential national organisation capable of safeguarding the sport of wildfowling, wildfowl and their habitat, then their future would be in serious jeopardy.

Today, however, the B.A.S.C. is concerned with and working for ALL aspects of sporting shooting, conservation and wildlife and the countryside as well as the lawful protection of quarry species, their habitat and the future well-being of the countryside in general.

In January 1975 the Gamekeepers' Association of the United Kingdom became incorporated within this Association.

*For further information please write to:*

The Director,
The B.A.S.C.,
Marford Mill,
Rossett, Wrexham,
Clwyd LL12 0HL.

Telephone : Rossett (STD 0244) 570881.

*Cover picture by Pamela Harrison*

# Know Your Woodpigeon Shooting

*by DENIS GRAHAM-HOGG*

*Photographs by*
Pamela Harrison, F.R.P.S.

John Marchington
Denis Graham-Hogg
John Harris

*Line drawings by*
John Paley

*First Published 1977*
*Revised edition 1978*


Marford Mill,
Rossett, Clwyd.

*Printed by*

*The Caxton & Holmesdale Press, Sevenoaks, Kent.*

# Know Your Woodpigeon Shooting

## Introduction

There is little recorded history of pigeons in Great Britain, but as a culinary bird we know that it was relished by the Romans. There is ample evidence provided by old dove cotes and pigeon lofts to suggest that pigeons were bred in large numbers from the Middle Ages onwards, either as ornamental birds or more probably for the table.

As a sporting bird the pigeon was either ignored or not present in large enough numbers to be worth the efforts of the shooting fraternity until the very end of the nineteenth century. When Colonel Peter Hawker died in 1853 he had only recorded 20 woodpigeons in his diaries covering the 51 years of his shooting career. However 40 years later woodpigeons were beginning to be a pest to farmers. Sir Ralph Payne-Gallwey in his Letters to Young Shooters series 1 (1890) says: 'We have numbers, I may say thousands of woodpigeon every winter, but a few shots, and they go, and we scarcely get a couple of score in the season'. However, in his second series published in 1892, Payne-Gallwey devotes no less than 37 pages to woodpigeon shooting, and it is true to say that nearly all the advice he gives on decoying and roost shooting is just as relevant today as it was when he wrote it over 90 years ago.

*The shooter's quarry. Columba palumbus. The Woodpigeon.*
*He fills his crop twice a day and eats the equivalent of his own weigh every four days.* *Photo:* John Marchington

**Identification**

Five species of pigeons are found in Great Britain, together with the familiar domestic variety. The shooters main quarry will usually be the Woodpigeon, *Columba palumbus*. Also known as the 'Cushat' or 'Cushy Doo' in Scotland, and the 'Quest' or 'Quist' in Wales.

It is the biggest of the five species, distributed over the whole of the British Isles, and tends to congregate more in intensive arable farming districts than in dairy or sheep farming areas.

In the adult bird there is no discernible difference between the sexes, and the distinguishing features are white bars on the wings and white neck patches. Immature birds less than three months old lack these neck patches and may be confused with the STOCK DOVE, which is smaller and has no white wing bars. Both birds have an overall grey body colour and a slightly rufous breast. They have the same feeding habits and are very gregarious, feeding in flocks sometimes numbering several hundreds.

The ROCK DOVE is the ancestor of the domestic pigeon, and is seen mainly round rocky coasts. It is protected everywhere and can be distinguished from the Stock Dove by grey wing tips and black wing bars and a white patch on the rump, and from the Woodpigeon also by the lack of white wing bars and the white neck patches. Under the Wildlife and Countryside Act 1981 the Stock Dove was given protection and now may NOT be shot at anytime in Great Britain.

The remaining two species are the Collared Dove and the Turtle Dove. The COLLARED DOVE spread to these islands from the continent in 1952 and in some parts of the country it is present in large numbers. It has ash-brown plumage, with a delicate pink body and a black collar. The underside of the tail is black with white tips.

When this booklet was first produced in the early part of 1977 the Collared Dove was a protected species in England and Wales and could not be shot, but it was not protected in Scotland. In some areas in England numbers had increased almost to pest proportions, particularly where it had colonised farm buildings, grain storage plants and silos. It causes damage by fouling grain and fodder crops stored inside buildings, by stealing grain put out by poultry breeders, game farmers and wildfowl/game collectors for penned and free flying birds, and in some urban areas it devastates kitchen gardens.

In March 1977 the Home Secretary made an order in Council transferring the Collared Dove to the Second Schedule of the Protection of Birds Act 1954, with respect to England and Wales. The Collared Dove, therefore from 1st April, 1977, was no longer protected and like the Woodpigeon may be shot at any time by authorised persons. This status was maintained with the introduction of the Wildlife and Countryside Act 1981.

The flesh is as good to eat as that of a Woodpigeon but the

*Choosing where and how to shoot.*

*Photo:* Denis Graham-Hogg

*Clothes which blend well with the surroundings make it unnecessary to use a hide. In this case a hat and mittens would give added concealment.*

*Photo:* John Marchington

Doves are much smaller, and therefore some people do not bother to shoot them. If you do decide to shoot them make sure your quarry identification is accurate since the TURTLE DOVE like the Collared Dove is present in some areas in fairly large numbers. It is generally darker and smaller than the Collared Dove with delicate chestnut coloured underparts, and a black and white patch on either side of the neck. It is protected in all areas and under no circumstances may it be shot.

Both Collared and Turtle Doves have rather a clipped, jerky flight which is easily distinguishable from the steady wing beats of the Woodpigeon. As the Woodpigeon is a much larger bird there is no excuse for shooting a Turtle Dove in mistake for a Woodpigeon.

When out Woodpigeon shooting, do not shoot if you are not quite certain of the species. Look for the white wing bars and the neck patches of the Woodpigeon. Under the Wildlife and Countryside Act 1981 the only pigeon species which may be sold dead are the Woodpigeon and Feral Pigeon.

## Choosing Where and How to Shoot

Woodpigeons can be shot all the year round and the two main methods are Roost Shooting and Decoying. The method you choose will depend on the time of year, the availability of food supplies, and the type of countryside over which you have permission to shoot. A good intelligence system between you the shooter, and landowners, farmers, gamekeepers and farm hands will save you hours of fruitless and frustrating waiting, and will increase your bag.

Reconnaisance with a pair of good binoculars will save you a lot of fruitless days when the pigeons are not where your informant told you they were. This last point can not be stressed too strongly and any pigeon shooter who fails to reconnoitre his ground only has himself to blame if sport is poor.

## Flight or Roost Shooting

Roost shooting is mainly a winter activity, and can be enjoyed in any piece of woodland or copse where pigeons roost at night or rest in the daytime. It is essential that you get under the flight line. A change of wind will cause birds to alter their line of approach and often their actual roosting place, and a few minutes studying where the birds are coming from and where they are actually landing will save you moving about to pick a better spot when you should be shooting.

If you pin-point the flight line and roosting spots it will be seldom necessary to make a hide, or if you do have to screen yourself because undergrowth is very sparse a very rudimentary screen of branches will be all that is necessary. Wear clothes that blend well with your surroundings, and a hat or peaked cap which covers the whiteness of your forehead, and stand with your back to a tree

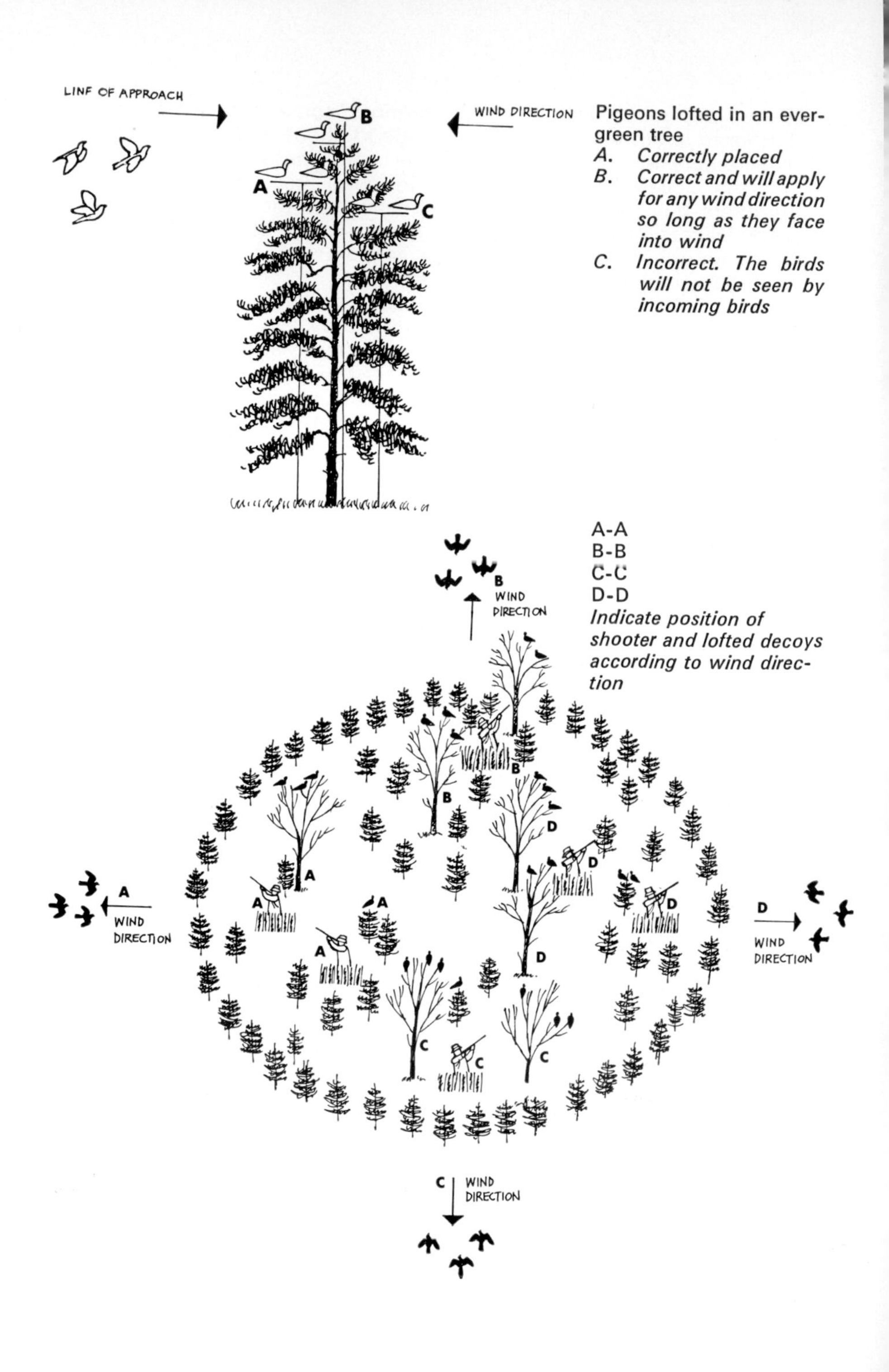


Pigeons lofted in an evergreen tree

*A. Correctly placed*

*B. Correct and will apply for any wind direction so long as they face into wind*

*C. Incorrect. The birds will not be seen by incoming birds*

A-A
B-B
C-C
D-D

*Indicate position of shooter and lofted decoys according to wind direction* or surrounded by bushes. This will give you all the cover you need, so long as you keep absolutely still until you raise your gun to fire.

In all forms of pigeon shooting absolute stillness is necessary as the birds are approaching. This cannot be stressed too strongly, as it is always movement of some kind which the incoming birds spot, to make them turn away well out of range, or jink with a turn and an incredible acceleration which will test the finest shot, and cause the average shot to miss time after time.

For added concealment some shooters advocate the use of a face mask and mittens, but a mask is most uncomfortable and it may impair your vision. If you are unfortunate enough to have to wear glasses you will find a mask more of a hindrance than a help. Keeping still and choosing clothes which blend with the background, and a hat which covers your forehead and ears are the most important things to consider.

**Decoys in a Wood**

Lofted decoys set in trees can be a great help in drawing birds near your hiding place. In effect the decoys allay suspicion when birds coming in to roost see other birds already sitting in the trees that they are making for. Pigeons, like any other wild creature, will choose whenever possible a sheltered resting place. It follows therefore that they will roost near the down-wind side of a wood, and are unlikely to decoy to birds placed near the upwind side.

If a wood is mainly fir and evergreens the decoys must be raised right to the top of the trees on the side from which the pigeons are approaching. If placed on the upwind side they will not be seen as the birds come in.

On the other hand, in a deciduous wood, the decoy's body can be seen through the bare branches. In this case the choice of trees is more important than trying to loft decoys on the down-wind side.

For some reason unknown to us humans, pigeons have favourite roosting trees. There may be two dozen trees in a radius of 100 yards which look all the same to human eyes, but the pigeons will choose three or four of those trees in preference to the others for their initial landing point, and only careful reconnaisance will tell us which those trees are.

Generally pigeons roost in the lower branches not more than about 20 feet from the ground, however they will often alight in a higher tree before dropping down to the final roosting place. Try as far as possible to place yourself where you can shoot through a gap in the trees, particularly in evergreen woodland. Amongst deciduous trees a gap is desirable but not absolutely imperative, as one can swing through the target ignoring the branches. This technique takes quite a lot of getting used to since we all subconsciously prefer a clear shot, but in fact small branches and twigs seem to have little effect on the shot pattern, and provided you swing normally a kill will result.

*Everyone should use a dog. Note the face mask and mittens giving added concealment.*

***Photo:*** John Marchington

The illustration opposite shows how in quite a small wood there are numerous possibilities for the positions of guns and decoys, depending on the wind direction.

**Retrieving in Woodland**

The B.A.S.C. advocates the use of a dog in all forms of shooting. Not only is a dog a wonderful companion which can give the genuine sportsman endless pleasure, but also by using a dog we leave far fewer dead or wounded birds unpicked. There is no point in shooting if you do not pick up your bag, and in woodland picking up without a dog can be very difficult.

You do not need a highly trained field trial dog for this type of shooting, rather one with a good nose and which marks well, for he or she will increase your total bag considerably. In open woodland incoming pigeons will take little or no notice of a dog running about, and in thick cover they will not see it anyway, so let the dog pick up as you shoot. Dogs cannot count and if you are getting a fair amount of shooting you will forget where your birds have dropped after you have got half a dozen or so down, so let the dog retrieve the birds as they fall, concentrating on the ones which drop some distance from you.

If you have no dog, picking up as you shoot will mean that you will get less shooting because by walking about as birds are coming in many will see you and will shy away. But even this is preferable to waiting till the end and then not being able to find many of your dead birds and virtually all which may have been wounded. If you want to get maximum enjoyment from shooting; use a dog.

**When to Stop**

Finally a word of advice on when to stop shooting. In woodland stop while birds are still coming in to roost. This means stopping when there is still plenty of light. Pigeons will make several attempts to come in to their chosen roost but if harried enough and frequently they will leave it altogether. No sensible sportsman wants this to happen so let the late-comers fly in in peace. There is always another day and by managing your shooting in a sensible and sportsmanlike manner the same piece of woodland can offer you sport throughout the whole winter.

Another aspect to think about is the effect late shooting has on roosting pheasants. If you go banging about in a wood as it gets dark pheasants will not go up to roost, or will leave the covert for a quieter resting place. If they roost on the ground they are easy prey for foxes and other predators, and no gamekeeper or landowner will thank you if his pheasants disappear after he has heard you shooting in his woods in the late evening.

---

*When looking for dead birds in woodland—*
*Do not forget to look up.*
*Photo:* John Marchington

## An indication of different types of food favoured by Woodpigeons during the agricultural year

| | |
|---|---|
| October<br>November<br>December | Wheat and barley on unploughed stubbles. Rape, clover beech mast and acorns. As the stubbles are ploughed rape and clover become more important. In the eastern counties sugar beet crumbs left behind after mechanical harvesting are much favoured. If there is early snow, kale, sprouts, rape or any green crops not blanketed will become the staple diet. |
| January<br>February<br>March | Clover and Lucerne and in snowy conditions. Rape, kale, sprouts, or any other green crop uncovered. Ivy berries, holly berries and frosted potatoes are also taken. |
| April<br>May<br>June | Spring sown wheat, barley, peas, beans and maize. Clover and any young sprouting plants such as kale, mustard, rape ,and turnips. Sprouting peas and kale should be particularly watched |
| July<br>August<br>September | Clover, young kale, mustard, grass seeds, then on to laid corn, ripe peas, soft fruits in fruit growing areas, and finally on to wheat and barley stubbles and where grown, ripe maize. In high summer some adult birds will not leave their woodland nesting sites, but will fill their crops with woodland and hedgerow leaves during the day. They may slip out for a late feed on the stubbles in the evening. |

*Setting out decoys for a bale hide on stubble.*
*Photo:* John Marchington

## Decoy Shooting

*The Pigeon's Diet*

For the majority of pigeon shooters decoying, as opposed to roost shooting, is the main sport. Whereas roost shooting is mainly a winter and early spring sport, decoying can be enjoyed all the year round and depends only on the food available.

A knowledge of pigeon diet, coupled with a good reconnaisance, are the two prerequisites for successful decoying. Pigeons, being very gregarious birds, tend to feed in flocks and a knowledge of what crops are being grown in any particular area, combined with a general knowledge of their preference for different foods at different times of the year, enables the shooter to get on terms with them in almost any month.

The table opposite gives an indication of what you may expect the birds to be feeding on at different times of the year, but a local knowledge of agricultural practices in your particular area will enable you to predict fairly accurately where they are likely to be congregating.

One cannot be dogmatic as to months or crops since our climate varies considerably, and crops in one part of the country may be a month in front of the same crop in another part, but pigeons, unless driven out of an area by very adverse weather conditions, tend to remain within a 20 or 30 mile radius of where they were hatched, so local knowledge of cropping programmes is most important.

*When pigeons feed and where to look for them*

A few years ago one used to hear that it was necessary to be out at dawn in order to get good pigeon shooting, but experienced shooters realise that this only applies when you do not know where the birds are feeding in the winter months. Pigeons will fill their crops twice a day, and in the winter with only a few hours of daylight, they make an early start and feed all day. If you do not know where they are feeding but know their roosting woods, you will have to be out very soon after dawn with a pair of binoculars to see in which direction they leave the roost. When you have spotted a number of birds going the same way you must drive as near as possible to where they disappeared and pick up the flight line again. After doing this a couple of times you will trace them to the field they are using.

In summer, with many more daylight hours they do not need to feed with such urgency as in winter and will tend to stay in the roosting areas until the sun is up and has dried the dew and warmed the air, and often 9 o'clock or 9.30 is quite early enough to start operations. In summer when there is much more food available they may readily change from one field to another. In the last few years this has become particularly noticeable, perhaps because pigeon shooting has become the main sport of a very large number of people. In some areas where pigeons have been harassed mercilessly they will leave a field very quickly after being shot at a few times, and split up into small parties feeding in many different fields.

When feeding on grain in the summer pigeons get very thirsty and will frequently fly to ponds, rivers, streams and even water troughs for a drink. Sometimes these watering places can give excellent shooting. Seldom will the sport be fast and furious, but when the weather is hot you can usually rely on a steady trickle of birds coming in all day.

A change of wind direction during the day may cause birds to change to a different field and the shooter should bear this in mind if birds suddenly stop coming to the field he has chosen. The only thing to do in this case is to do a reconnaisance and to pin-point the new feeding areas. Pigeons are greedy birds and this can be their undoing. If there is a suitable field under a flight line into a roost, a few decoys put out after about 5.30 in the evening will often tempt birds going in to roost to stop for a last few mouthfuls, and sport can go on until 7.30 or as late as 8 o'clock.

There are few hard and fast rules about decoying. Only reconnaisance and careful watching and noting of movement will tell you in which field or fields you should operate, but as a general guide the greater the number of pigeons using a field, the more likely they are to stay there throughout the day. They may fly off to drink or rest, but rest assured they will return to fill their crops.

*Siting your Hide*

If you ever get the opportunity to go out decoying with an expert, take a note of how much trouble he takes to decide exactly where to place his hide. You will hear pigeon shooters say that they always like to have the wind behind them so that they get birds approaching head on, or that they prefer a going away shot, and they site their hide without taking anything else into consideration. This is not the way of the experienced shooter. Firstly he will note the flight line into the field, and secondly which part of the field is in favour on that particular day.

There will always be what we call a 'collecting' area some distance away which will determine the final flight line to the field. The collecting area may be a wood or a bunch of trees or even a few trees in a hedgerow, and it may be some distance from the field, as much as a mile or so away. Sometimes you may find that there are two collecting areas in use, particularly when the area is thickly wooded, and in this case there will be two flight lines coming in. The rule to follow is get under or as near as possible to a flight line.

In large fields, such as we find in the eastern counties of England, pigeons choose a particular part of a field in which to feed. It is by no means certain what governs this choice, but it probably has something to do with wind direction. Birds seldom choose an exposed area in a wind when a fold in the ground may give some protection. It follows that as well as studying the flight line you should also take into account the part of the field being favoured. You should also look for 'sitty' trees, for if there are some close to the flight line a hide placed within shot of them can pay handsomely.

The illustration shows a large field with three distinct collecting areas, each of which may be used in a different wind. It should be noted that there will be continual movement round the outer circle of the collecting areas. For instance when disturbed on feeding area 'A' birds will probably go out to collecting area 'B' or 'C' and then will make their way back to collecting area 'A' before coming in again.

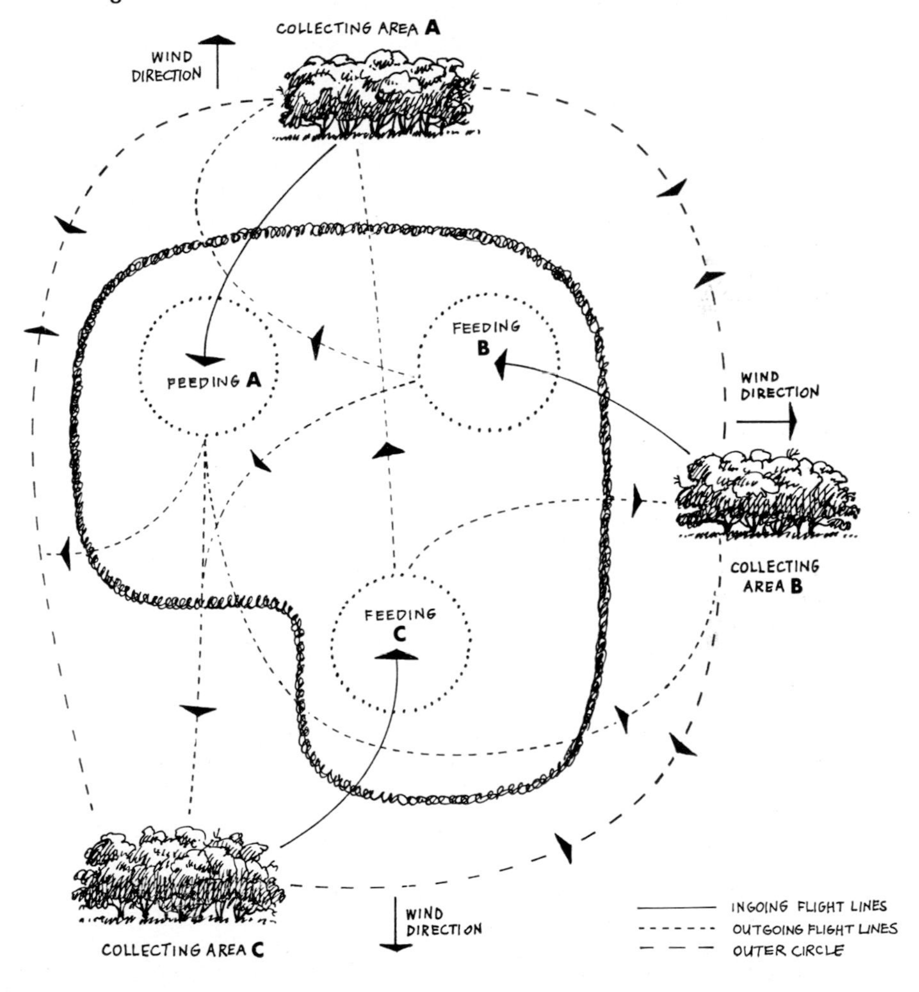

*Shooting from a bale hide. Note overhead cover* *Photo:* John Marchington

*A natural hedgerow hide in winter. Note the overhead cover* *Photo:* John Marchington

Although hides should always be placed below an incoming flight line, where this is not possible a hide below the outgoing line is second best. In this case you may have to be some distance from the feeding area, and you will really be flight shooting, as all your decoys will really be doing is channeling the birds out, and you will be relying on the sound of your shots disturbing the birds coming in to the feeding area. Where two guns are shooting the same field it should be possible to site one hide under the incoming line and one under the outgoing, and both guns will get good sport. Alternatively, if you have access to the collecting area you might consider placing a second gun here. Excellent shooting can result as the birds are kept on the move continually.

*Types of Hides and Equipment*

Having decided where to place your hide your next decision will be to choose the sort of hide you wish to use. Your final choice will depend on the cover which is available and the time of year.

Out in an open field a bale hide can be very effective and it has the advantage that it can be used several times if a few minutes are spent on maintaining it, and it can be made very comfortable and wind proof.

Where bales are not available hessian or camouflage netting can be used. Hessian is light to transport and is particularly suitable when the hide has to be placed out in the open on a newly sown corn field. Four corner posts will be necessary and these can either be stout ones which are rammed into the ground, or slender tent pole type of posts which are light to carry and can be erected with guy ropes. One often sees hessian hides left out in the field during the spring sowing and it is not uncommon for a shooter to erect two or three of these hides in the same field, so that the favourite feeding areas are all covered.

Most pigeon shooters carry camouflage netting as part of their normal equipment. Ex-army netting made of heavy string and hessian is readily available very cheaply, but it has the great draw-back that it is very bulky and heavy. A 15ft. x 5ft. net of this type weighs about 15lbs. and double that when wet, and when a shooter is laden with net, poles, guns, cartridges, picnic lunch, flask, decoys and something to sit on, he is probably carrying about 40lbs., and looks like an Everest porter. After carrying this lot across a couple of ploughed fields, he begins to wonder if it is worth it. In the last few years netting made of thin nylon string and plastic 'leaves' has come on the market, and though a good deal more expensive than the older type of netting the expenditure is well worth while. A 15ft. x 5ft. length of this netting weighs less than 1½lbs., and can be rolled up in a tight bundle which will go in a haversack, game bag, or even a hare pocket. In addition it does not

*The new and the old type of netting. A comparison of 2 x 15ft. lengths.*
*The new netting with an artificial decoy gives an indication of the lack of bulk.*

*Photo:* Denis Graham-Hogg

*Netting and natural cover. Note the shooting 'window'.* *Photo:* John Marchington

*A natural hedgerow hide in summer.*
*Note the sun flash on the glasses and the bare left forearm.*

*Photo:* Denis Graham-Hogg

absorb water and even if left wet it will not rot. Telescopic aluminium poles are replacing metal rods, and these also are much lighter to carry and easier to transport.

Probably the most common type of hide in use is a combination of camouflage netting and natural foliage.

Where the hide is to be made in the edge of a wood or a thick hedgerow, a natural hide is easy to make with the foliage available. For this purpose a small bill-hook, a largish knife or a small sickle should be part of the equipment of every pigeon shooter.

In the eastern counties fields are intersected by deep ditches or dykes. When they are dry often all that is necessary is for the shooter to get down into the ditch, cut a seat out of the bank behind him, a shelf in the bank in front, adjust the grass and foliage in front of him and he is in business.

In stock raising areas post and rail fences are common and these often have little natural foliage which can be used. A hessian hide with rails painted across it is extremely effective and some shooters will even paint the hessian green between the rails to give the appearance of grass.

Whatever type of hide you use make sure that you make it roomy. Nothing is more conducive to bad shooting than being uncomfortable and having to restrict your swing, or not being able to move your feet because your dog is in the way as he has nowhere else to go. Cover over the top of the hide is preferable to an open top. If you have planned your decoy pattern to give you a good killing area in front of the hide you will not need to shoot birds passing overhead. With a cover they can fly all round the hide and you will not be seen.

Some people do not like shooting sitting down, but this is only a matter of practice. Try and train yourself to be able to do this rather than to have to stand up to shoot over the top of the front of the hide. Standing up every time you shoot means movement, and as we have already said when referring to roost shooting, movement is the first thing a pigeon will spot, and you will scare many birds if you are up and down like a jack-in-the-box.

The B.A.S.C. and the Game Conservancy now sell an ideal hide seat in the form of a shortened shooting stick. Known as the "T seat" it is made of plastic, folds up and is light to carry. Folded it can clip on your belt, gun sling or cartridge bag and is another must for shooting over decoys. It is also ideal incidentally for the Game Shooter waiting at his peg for a drive to start or for anyone in the countryside who may not wish to sit on the wet grass.

The position of the sun must be taken into account when building your hide. It is preferable to have the sun to one side or behind you, because shooting into the sun is difficult particularly when it is low in the afternoon, and with the sun shining straight into your hide the birds will see movement much more easily. Glasses can be a great drawback when the sun is in front of you, as the lenses act as reflectors, and just as a lighthouse warns a ship of danger, so will flashing glasses warn pigeons to keep well clear. If you have to shoot into the sun which is sometimes unavoidable, a large covered hide with a good window to shoot through will solve your problem.

## Decoys and Setting Them Out

There are a number of artificial decoys on the market, all of which can do an adequate job. Some of them when looked at closely do not resemble woodpigeons very much but at a distance they have the general outline and colour of pigeons. These will attract birds from a distance, but often on nearer approach pigeons see that something is wrong and steer clear of the decoys.

There is no doubt at all that dead birds set up as decoys do a better job of attracting your quarry than the artificial decoys, but when dead birds, either stuffed or from a previous day's shooting are not available, artificials are the next best thing.

If you are doing a lot of shooting it is worthwhile making dead birds you have shot into "real" decoys. Details of how to do this are on pages 31 & 32, and after a little practice the beginner can become quite an expert at simple taxidermy, and can make excellent decoys from freshly shot birds. With careful handling these "real" decoys will last at least two seasons, but you must keep them out of the way of children as they are impregnated with formaldehyde. This is a solution of formalin which is a poison, and therefore the kit must be kept locked up or on a high shelf if you have children and animals in the house.

Alternatively you can select a dozen birds in good condition after a day's shooting, and put them in the freezer for your next outing. This is rather an expensive way of using dead birds particularly in the summer, as they soon go off as they thaw out, and have to be thrown away at the end of the day. In winter if the weather is cold they may still be fresh enough to eat or to go to the dealer, but there is always the risk that a dealer will reject birds which have been frozen and thawed out.

Whether you use artificial decoys or the real thing, you will probably not be able to carry enough to the field to give you an ideal decoy pattern. Most shooters start off with anything from eight to about 15 decoys and add dead birds to the cluster as they shoot them. This should be done when you have several birds down and as soon as there is a lull in the shooting. When you leave the hide to set up decoys, leave your gun after unloading it, in the hide. You will not then be tempted to have pot shots at birds which may try and come in while you are setting up. The quicker you can get out, set up and back in the hide again the better. If you can set your dead bird up on a small mound of earth all the better, and on clover or in stubble a clod of earth or a bunch of straw will do.

*The real thing and artificials.*
*The 'real' birds have been preserved and set up using the WAGBI Kit,*
*and have been in use for nearly a year.*
*Note the unnatural shine on the artificial birds.* *Photo:* Denis Graham-Hogg

*A simple trolley. The handles and wheel are removable for easy transport in the car. Without a trolley our shooter would look like an Everest porter.*
*Photo:* Denis Graham-Hogg

*Pigeons feeding facing in all directions.* *Photo:* John Marchington

*Setting up a decoy with spread wings on kale.*

*Photo:* John Marchington

Prop the head up with a pointed stick pressed into the head behind the beak, and vary the position of the head.

If you see a pigeon alert to danger you will note that it is standing with its neck stretched upwards with the body poised for a quick jump into the air. Feeding pigeons look relaxed and when setting up you should try and make the decoy look as relaxed as possible. Some can be in a pecking position, others can have the heads turned to one side or the other and yet others can be set with the breast puffed out and the head set down on the shoulders as though the birds are relaxing and almost asleep. A couple of dozen birds with their necks all stretched out and heads pointing up into the air will be a first class danger signal to incoming birds.

Some people advocate a forked stick to prop up the head, but a pointed stick is simpler and does the job just as well. Other people swear by wire cradles to prop up the whole bird, but these are very bulky to carry and you will have quite enough equipment to haul around without adding to it. The only situation in which a wire cradle might be useful is on green crops such as kale in the winter, or on laid corn, but even in these cases artificial decoys set up above the crop on long sticks probably do just as well, and on laid corn a dead bird or two can be put on bunches of straw above the laid area.

If you do use wire cradles count them when you leave to make sure none are left in the crop. The farmer will not thank you if you leave one and it smashes up the cutter bar of his combine or forage harvester when he is harvesting.

Seldom if ever will you need more than about 35 to 40 decoys out, and when this number has been reached you can stop adding to the pattern. Circumstances will dictate the number you use since if you find that 20 or 25 decoys are attracting a steady stream of shootable birds, it is obviously a waste of time setting out more when you could be adding to the bag.

---

*On laid corn the decoy should be set up as high as possible so that it can be seen from a distance.* *Photo:* John Marchington

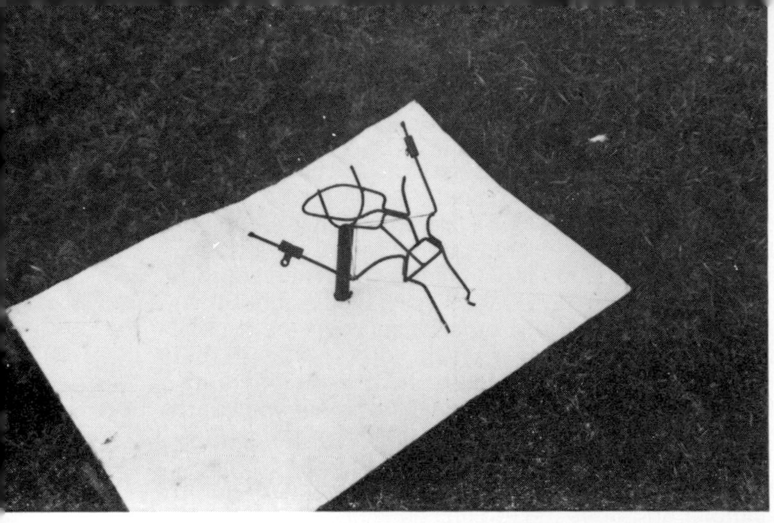

*A flapper in use: The craddle-and wire for the line*

*The flapper at rest.*

*Photos:* Denis Graham Hogg

*Flapping Note: This was an immature bird, indicated by lack of the white neck ring.*

Decoys should not be placed too close together. A distance of about 9 to 10 feet between birds is quite close enough. All birds land into wind, but once they start feeding, unless the wind is very strong they face in all directions, except directly tail to wind, so do not set out your decoys like a platoon of guardsmen, all facing the front. Vary the direction they face with one or two pointing three-quarters down wind.

### Using a 'Flapper'

We have said that movement on the part of the shooter will be spotted by incoming birds and will quickly warn them of danger, but movement by other pigeons usually has the reverse effect. For this reason many experts use a 'flapper' decoy to attract birds and there is no doubt that a flapper somewhere near the centre of the decoy pattern will bring in many birds which would otherwise ignore the decoys. The equipment needed is quite simple as illustrated opposite.

A WAGBI/Semark cradle to hold a dead bird, and about 50 yards of strong non-stretch nylon line. The line bricklayers use is ideal.

If a fresh shot bird is used the wing bones must be broken as near to the body as possible. If this is not done rigor mortis sets in and the wings will not flap. If a bird from the fridge is used after thawing out its only necessary to loosen the wing joints nearest to the body. Breaking is not necessary as the joints will not stiffen up again. Details of the flapper are shown inside the back cover.

Since this flapper was developed some years ago by Sid Semark in conjunction with the author of this booklet it has proved so successful that a number of copies have been put on the market by other manufacturers so beware of imitations.

As a pigeon lands it flaps its wings very fast about five or six times to break its speed just above the ground. The head is well up and the feet thrust forward for landing. Having landed it pauses for about two or three seconds then gives one quick flap of the wings to get all its feathers comfortable. The object of the 'flapper' is to give the impression of a pigeon landing, so when you see birds which are not coming to the decoys but are passing the field, pull the line very fast about six times, pause, and then give one more quick pull. Birds some distance away will often see the movement and will turn from their flight line to investigate. Do not use the 'flapper' when birds are close and obviously coming in to the decoy pattern.

### The Decoy Pattern

When deciding on your decoy pattern the direction of the wind must be taken into consideration. A gap in the pattern can be left directly in front of the hide and this is what we can call the killing area. If a 'flapper' is being used this should be on the edge of the killing area. The bulk of the decoys should be in a circle within 35 yards from the hide, and you can place a few birds to form a 'lead in' and a 'lead out' of the decoy pattern. This is particularly useful when you are shooting near a tall hedge or high trees, and lead in birds can be placed on the other side of the hedge or the trees, to attract birds which otherwise would not see the main decoy pattern. If the wind is directly from the front, the pattern will have to be fairly tight and the nearest decoys to the hide may have to be as close as 10 yards in order to get the birds down to the killing area before they are out of range. The illustrations opposite show typical decoy patterns for various wind directions.

## Shooting from the Hide

One of the mistakes the beginner makes when hide shooting is to be too eager and to take difficult shots which are unnecessary. A high percentage of kills to cartridges used can be achieved if you refrain from shooting at any bird unless it is over the killing area. If a bird gives a difficult chance and does not come right in, let it go. It will most likely circle round and come in a second time and give you a much easier shot. If two or more birds come in together let one land if they look as though they want to, then take the bird following as it comes in, and you will get a nice chance to shoot the bird which has landed as it takes off in a hurry.

Get used to shooting sitting down. A five gallon oil drum, with an old sack for padding, makes an ideal seat. Keep your gun barrels down inside the hide. Often one sees a shooter well concealed from incoming birds but with two feet of gun sticking out above the hide. It is all too easy when you are crouching down, to forget that your gun barrels are waving about above your head.

Leave peep holes through which you can watch for birds flying behind you or on each side, but do not try to use these for shooting through, they are merely there so that you will not be taken by surprise by birds you had not seen coming in to the decoys.

## Picking Up

Do not try to pick up every bird as you shoot it, but wait until there is a lull then get out and back as quickly as possible. A dog can be very useful and hide shooting is good training for a young dog. Make it stay in the hide and get used to waiting until told to retrieve. Pick up most of the easy retrieves yourself, and make the young dog stay in the hide while you do this. All birds which drop some distance away can be collected by your dog, and he will save you a lot of walking. A young dog will try and pick up birds which you have just set up as decoys, but a sharp 'no' or 'leave it' will stop him, and it will not be too long before your dog learns that birds with the scent of your hands on them must not be touched.

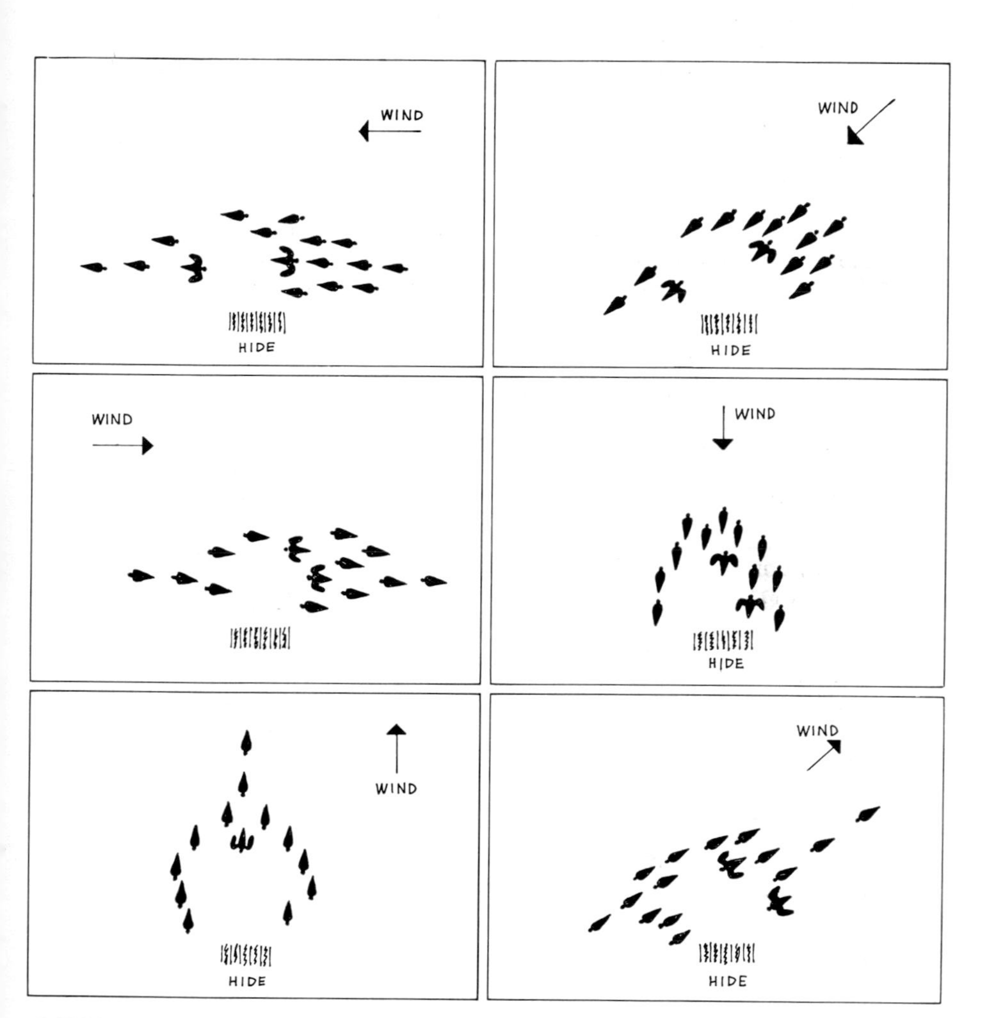


*LAYOUTS FOR DECOYS and FLAPPER*

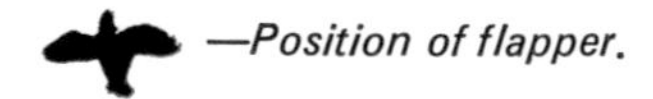

*—Position of flapper.*

Note: *There is often more than one choice for the position of the flapper.*

During the spring and early summer do not let your dog hunt the hedgerows for lost birds when partridges or pheasants are likely to be sitting on eggs, or raising chicks. If you are shooting on a keepered estate, the keeper should be able to tell you where birds are nesting, and you can make sure that you give them a wide berth.

**Shooting in the Game Season**

Many estates do not allow shooting near their woodlands during the pheasant season from October to the end of the following January. If you are lucky enough to get permission to shoot on an estate or farm where game is preserved do not let your dog disturb the woodlands, and keep away from them yourself if you possibly can. In any case if the estate is keepered always check with the keeper before you decide to shoot in a wood. He will not thank you if you go roost shooting in a wood the evening before he has planned to drive it for pheasants.

**General Behaviour**

Remember if you are not the owner of the land over which you shoot, you are there as the owner's or the tenant farmer's guest. Do not leave litter about which is not only unsightly but if eaten by stock can do serious damage. Young stock will eat almost anything, and ingested litter has been known to kill calves and adult stock.

Do not damage fences or leave gates open through which stock can stray, and if you are shooting towards a hedgerow make certain that there are no stock the other side of it which might get peppered.

If the farmer or keeper asks you to shoot rabbits and vermin, all well and good, but check with them first. They will probably be pleased if you shoot a stoat or a crow, but rabbits may be reserved for the farmer himself or the shooting tenant, so the rule is check first.

Keep your eyes open for signs of vermin, and this includes poachers. Tell the keeper or farmer what you see. The keeper can be your best friend or worst enemy, so anything you can do to help him, particularly in the breeding season will pay dividends.

**Guns and Cartridges**

Many people will have particular preferences for guns and loads, but if you follow the advice given in previous pages about placing hides and setting out decoys you will not need a heavily choked gun or heavy ammunition.

Nearly all your shots over decoys will be taken within 35 yards and most of them between 20 and 30 yards. At these ranges heavy chokes are a disadvantage, so an ordinary game gun with improved

*A dog will increase your enjoyment as well as your bag.* *Photo:* John Harris cylinder in the right barrel and quarter choke in the left will be quite adequate.

For some reason pigeons have got the reputation of being hard to kill and great shot carriers. This is probably because their feathers shed very easily and one pellet passing through the feathers and not actually touching the body will result in a cloud of feathers being left behind. In fact pigeons are not hard to kill, and No. 6 or 7 shot have quite enough penetration to kill cleanly and regularly. One ounce loads or ordinary game loads are used by most of the experts who find anything heavier than No. 6 quite unnecessary.

## Racing Pigeons

We would like to end this booklet with a word of warning.

The Racing Pigeon is protected by Law and to shoot it is an offence against that Law. The ready identification of the racing pigeon is therefore of paramount importance.

The Racing Pigeon carries a metal, or plastic covered metal, registration ring. In the case of rings issued by the Royal Pigeon Racing Association the details appearing thereon would be, for example, NU 75 A 12345—where NU indicates National Union (with effect from 1976 it will be G.B.—Great Britain), 75 the year of issue, and A 12345 the registration number. In addition, and when engaged in a race the pigeon would also carry one, or two, plastic/rubber garters which are coded and specific to that one pigeon and one race only. On arrival home the 'garter' would be removed and placed in a special timing clock which records the day, hour, minute and second of 'clocking in'.

Even when exercising round its home territory the identification of the Racing Pigeon should present little problem. In the first place there is the colour indication, for Racing Pigeons can be of any colour, whereas Woodpigeons are all cast in the same colour mould. During the racing season which commences in late March/ early April, and finishes at the end of October, the identification aspect is made even more simple, for during this period the appearance of the Woodpigeon in large tightly knit packs travelling fast and as straight as a gun barrel is not seen, as is the case with the Racing Pigeon. Even single Racing Pigeons fly straight—giving the appearance of knowing where they are going. When the wind is on their tails they will be travelling very fast and at a height, but when the wind is dead against them they will be virtually hedge-hopping.

Probably the greatest danger period for the 'odd' pigeon(s) is in June and July when engaged in races up to 600 miles, plus. Naturally after flying for many hours the pigeon is not as fresh as normal and could possibly be mistaken by a shooter. Here there is probably the greatest of all distinctions between the Woodpigeon and the Racing Pigeon; the Woodpigeon displays alarm and flinches away from the pointed gun, the Racing Pigeon does not. Particular care should therefore be exercised during June/July, because no shooting enthusiast would enjoy the shooting of a Racing Pigeon that had probably flown several hundreds of miles, only to be killed in the home straight, so to speak.

Let us respect and not interfere with the sport of others, just as we expect them to respect and not interfere with our sport of shooting.

The Headquarters of The Royal Pigeon Racing Association is 'The Reddings', Nr. Cheltenham, Glos., and the General Manager of the Association will be pleased to answer any queries you, the reader, might have.

---

*A typical racing pigeon. There can be a wide range of colour variation*

## Safety and Insurance

The final word must be about safety. However careful one is, and however long you have been shooting, accidents do happen.

In a court of law, the man who pulled the trigger, or who dropped the gun, or who left it unattended with a live cartridge in the breech, is the person who is responsible in the event of an accident happening.

Compensation these days is very heavy, and if not for your own sake, for the sake of the person who may be injured by **your** carelessness, everyone who carries a gun should be fully insured.

Every B.A.S.C. member is insured for a sum of £1,000.000 agains third party risk, for any one accident. This is automatic on becoming a member of B.A.S.C. Although there are many other reasons why all shooting people should join the Association which fights for their rights as sportsmen, the insurance alone makes it worthwhile, for where else will you get third party insurance cover for £1,000,000 for the price of a few boxes of cartridges.

## HOW TO MAKE NATURAL PIGEON DECOYS

The most effective decoys are made by stuffing dead pigeons. They are reasonably hardwearing and can last for at least six months even when used every week, but use in rain is not recommended.

With a little practice they can be produced in a few minutes.

The process is basically embalming, and requires much less skill than may appear from the following description :—

### Materials Required

Good freshly shot pigeons without broken wings.
Stiff wire – thin galvanised wire (e.g. 1.60 mm) is ideal.
Cotton wool or other stuffing.
Sharp knife – a pen knife is ideal.
Scissors.
Needle & thread.
Pliers.
Hypodermic syringe – the throw-away plastic type used by Doctors and Veterinary Surgeons is quite suitable and used syringes can often be obtained from them without charge. Please make sure it is kept out of reach of children.
Formaldehyde Solution ("Formalin") obtainable from Chemists. The standard solution usually supplied is about 40% and can be diluted with up to three times its volume of water. Strong solution cures the birds more quickly, but makes them much more brittle. Diluted solution takes longer to cure but produces a longer-lasting decoy. The solution is poisonous.

### Method

Work on a smooth shiny surface – "Formica" is ideal. Try to move the bird as little as possible during the "operation" to avoid dislodging feathers from the back.

1. Place the bird on its back, tail towards you. Part the breast feathers and cut the skin along the keel of the breast bone. Turn the skin back until the whole of the breast bone is clear. Cut off the feet and legs outside, skin the inner parts of the legs and cut them off close to the body.
2. Cut through the breast meat to the bone at each side close to the wing joints. Remove all the breast meat and give it to the cook.
3. Below the rear end of the breast bone make a hole in the skin to give access to the internal organs. Remove these with your fingers or a spoon. Clean out the inside of the carcase first with dry cotton wool then with a swab of cotton wool soaked in Formalin. Leave the swab inside the carcase then fill the cavity well with cotton wool, old newspapers or any suitable stuffing materials.
4. Using about 7 inches of wire, bend one end as shown overleaf and insert this doubled end up inside the neck alongside the spine, and force it into but not through the head. The rest of the wire is bent roughly along the line of the breast bone and pushed through the bone close to the rear end. It may be necessary to make a hole in the breast bone first. Bend the end of the wire back on itself and clamp the bend tight with pliers.

5. Inject, with the syringe about 1 ml. (the quantity is not critical) of the formaldehyde solution into the internal ends of the wing muscles, and into the wings above and below the elbow joint. Swab off the breast bone with cotton wool soaked in formalin, and leave half of the swab on each side of the breast bone.
6. Take two handfuls of cotton wool and fill the skin and carcase on each side of the breast. Use as much as you can conveniently get in, making the decoy as large as possible, as it will shrink when dry. Draw the edges of the skin together and join them with a few stitches.
7. Inject 1 ml. formaldehyde solution into the skull, inserting the needle gently through the back of the skull with a twisting movement.
8. Cut off the lower eyelids. Place the bird upright in the attitude required on a table or floor where it can remain for a fortnight, bending the neck as required and supporting the wings slightly away from the body on crumpled newspaper or cotton wool. Make the position as natural as possible, with the head not too high. Spread the tail and fix the outer feathers with drawing pins or adhesive tape.
9. In about a fortnight the decoy will have dried out, and should be completely rigid. It will, however, be somewhat brittle and should therefore be handled carefully. The lasting qualities can be improved by spraying the body with hair lacquer or a little light silicone compound.

### Notes

Formaldehyde is a poison, and can be dangerous if used in any other way than as directed. Avoid inhaling the vapour or splashing the solution, and keep it in labelled bottles out of the way of children and pets.

Formaldehyde solution cures your skin as well as the decoy, so use rubber gloves or some kind of tongs for handling it. If you do get it on the skin you will have to wait for it to wear off.

The decoys will be liable to damage by moth larvae if stored for any length of time, and it is advisable to keep "moth balls" or other moth repellant with them.

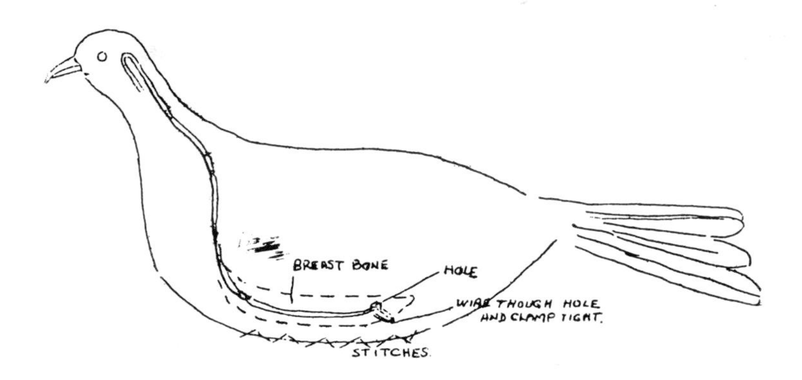